FLIGHT OF AN ANGEL

FLIGHT OF AN ANGEL

Dreams do come true

JIMMIE LEE HABERSHAM

authorHOUSE®

AuthorHouse™
1663 Liberty Drive
Bloomington, IN 47403
www.authorhouse.com
Phone: 1-800-839-8640

First published by AuthorHouse   11/23/2011

ISBN: 978-1-4678-6986-7 (sc)
ISBN: 978-1-4678-6985-0 (hc)
ISBN: 978-1-4678-6984-3 (ebk)

Library of Congress Control Number: 2011919814

Printed in the United States of America

TABLE OF CONTENTS

BIOGRAPHY

Jimmie Lee Habersham Jr. was born in Vidette Georgia. He resides in Pompano Beach Florida. He is a graduate of Blanche Ely High School. He attended Tuskegee University 1985-1987. He is a graduate from Barry University in 2006 with a B.S. degree in Health Service Administration. He is currently an associate minister at the Hopewell Missionary Baptist Church of Pompano Beach Florida. He serves as chairman of the Outreach Ministry, Chairman of the Adopt-a-Street Program, and Chairman of the Greif Ministry. He is a preacher and a teacher. He is married and has three children.

LIFE AS A CHILD

I was born in Louisville Georgia on May 7, 1963. I was born to the late Jimmie Lee and Alzora Cooper Habersham. To that union seven children were born. I am the fifth child out of a total of seven children. I am the only boy, and have six sisters. Two of my sisters have preceded me in death. Through the course of my life, I have always witnessed my mother struggle to make ends meet. My mama never made it past the sixth grade in school. She could not read and write as well as her younger siblings. Mama didn't have a job, so she would clean the house of many of the local residents for a few dollars and whatever leftover foods that they would give her. Because we couldn't afford a car, I remember her hitchhiking for rides to get to the neighboring city to work in others homes. Sometimes it would be dark before she returned home in the evening. She was referred to as a domestic worker. Some may call it being a maid, others may call it housekeeping. That was her profession. Sometimes with the little money that she made, she would always think of a way to provide for us children.

I remember mama ordering approximately fifty to one hundred baby chicks for a few months to raise for food. Many of the baby chicks did not survive therefore; she had to order them over again and again. The chickens were kept in the chicken yard with a chicken coop and a hen house. Once the chicks reached a certain size, we always had something to eat. We separated the roosters from the hens. Some of the hens were productive in laying eggs which was an added benefit. We also had a pigpen where we raised our own hogs. Whenever the sows would have pigs, my sisters and I would claim one for ourselves. We would challenge each other to see whose pig would grow the fastest. I had my own pig to feed and I named extra help stacking the bales as they were being tossed onto the trailer. After the day was over, I was tired and disappointed because I had lost my quarter in one of the haystacks. The last thing that I could remember doing as a young lad is hoeing weeds in a soybean field. I didn't have the opportunity to pick cotton, but I can imagine what it was like compared to hoeing weeds. Every hot summer morning, I would join my older sisters in the fields. Each of us would be assigned a row to hoe until we finished the field. I received many blisters on my hands from not knowing how to use a hoe. Sometimes it took us about a week to complete one field. While we were hoeing weeds, the crop dusters would be spraying the adjacent fields. There were many times that I was afraid of the planes, but I was fascinated when I saw them up close.

Getting older also caused me to get in a lot of trouble. One day my uncle Robert introduced me to smoking. I didn't like the idea of smoking. In order to get me to smoke, he would threaten me by saying that he would tell my mother or beat me. Smoking wasn't the only thing. I began to become mischievous because I was hanging out with guys that were older than I. They would try to influence me to do things that were wrong. Our favorite hangout spot was at one of the two local stores on Sunday evenings. We chose this particular store because the resident that lived near the other store was a police officer. There was the possibility of him driving up to the house at anytime. There were also a city park nearby that we could use as an alibi to what we were doing near the store. The stores were closed on Sundays due to the owners' religious beliefs and respect to the word of God. We would hang around the store every Sunday as a meeting place smoking and talking. One day they decided to break into the store and vandalized it. I was sort of a lookout and I was told not to tell anyone what had happened on that day. During the night, I could not sleep because this was troubling me.

The next morning I went to school as if nothing had happened. While in school, I was summoned to come to the principal's office over the intercom system. When I approached the office I saw the police officer in the principal's office. He was waiting for me at the door. He had a cast of what appeared to be my footprint in his hand. The police officer told me that they knew that I was at the scene because my foot prints were all around the store and my finger prints were on the soda machines. He asked me some questions about what happened at the store. I didn't tell him anything because my uncle had already threatened to beat me up if I told. We were all caught and had to go before the local magistrate. My uncle and the others guys were put on probation. Because of my age, I was told not to hang out with those fellows again. The guys became mad at me because they thought that I was the one that told everything.

Another day came where I was involved with the same guys getting into trouble. One day we went into one of the local residents watermelon patch. The melons were ripe and ready to be gathered. We sneaked into the patch and began to smash as many watermelons as we possibly could without getting caught. We also ate some as well. It was more like a vendetta against the owner. A couple of days later, the resident came over to my house and ask me to come go with him rabbit hunting. I didn't know that he was going to ask me questions about what happened at the store and if I knew who did it. His comments to me were, "A bunch of boys went into my melon patch and smashed almost all my melons. Do you know who did it? My response was that I didn't know, knowing all the time that I was part of that bunch. Then, he saw a rabbit at the edge of the road about fifty yards ahead of us. He told me that he could hit him right between the eyes. As we traveled a little farther down the road, we spotted another rabbit running in a field. The rabbit stopped and all you could see was his ears in the underbrush. He said that he could hit him right between the ears. Both rabbits were shot exactly where he said he would hit them. Maybe this was his way of intimidating me to expose what I knew about the smashing of the watermelons. There is no doubt in my mind that he was an expert shooter. But what troubled me was the fact that if he was angry, it could have been me he was hunting! No one would have ever known what had happened to me. I thank God that Mr. Roland had a compassionate heart.

I also became disobedient to my mother. My mother and father did not get along very well. There were times when she talk about being bullied and picked on everyday while in school. I sympathize for them because I know firsthand about what they are going through. I thank God for watching over me. As I look back over my life as a child, there is no doubt in my mind that God had placed his angels around me.

THE UNTOLD SECRET

When I was about eleven years old, I was physically abused by my oldest sister. This went on periodically for about a year. I can recall one night waking up feeling her hands on my private area. As I pushed them away, she began to threaten me. She told me that if I told anyone she was going to beat me up. As if I didn't have enough problems, this one sort of took the cake. I went into withdrawal as though nothing really happened. I felt shameful, I felt as if I was useless, most of all, I felt as if no one cared about me. How can my sister do something like that to me? I trusted her and looked up to her because she was my big sister. Whenever my mother would leave home, she left her in charge of us because she was the oldest. It was during those times that she would try to take advantage of me. But, because of my ruggedness, I always put up a good fight. This is what really kept her from advancing. I didn't understand what was going on, but I remember it stopped when the older teenage boys would come by the house.

I have often heard of sexual abuse from family members on different TV programs. Incest among siblings is very real. Incest can be defined as having sexual contact with a family member such as a brother, sister, uncle, or even your aunt. It can start by making verbal explicit comments, to actually having sexual intercourse. Sometimes I would just sit and listen when victims would share their experience with various people. As I listened carefully, I could remember some of those very things happening to me. I felt just like so many other countless victims that I did not report it to my mother. Not only did I feel shameful, but I think that is what may have caused me to be so defensive. I felt like I had to prove everything to everyone. Even as I speak today, sometimes I feel like I am sitting on a bunch of needles or standing on egg shells. I have become analytical in my thinking. I carefully examine things that are being said, or, I try not to engage in conversations that have no relevant meaning. I was emotionally abused as well as physically abused. What does it mean to be emotionally abused? According to The National Council on Child Abuse, emotional abuse is the most difficult form of child abuse to verify. It includes both verbal assaults and the withholding of positive emotional support. Although the scars may not be visible to the naked eye, emotional abuse wounds the spirit, frequently leaving its marks for a lifetime.

Victims of emotional abuse are "hit" every day with the power of words which are demeaning, shaming, threatening, blaming, intimidating, unfairly critical or sarcastic in nature. This form of abuse is destructive to a child's self-confidence and self-esteem. It can affect a child's emotional development, resulting in a sense of worthlessness and inadequacy. Some indicators of potential emotional abuse include: Patterned behavior that is extreme (e.g., lying, stealing, fighting) or is overly aggressive and acts out inappropriately; Appears defensive, shy or overly dependent;

The NCAA (National Council on Child Abuse) also states that incidents of child sexual abuse are damaging whether they occur only once, are repeated many times, or last over a number of years. A single, seemingly minor incident, (e.g. indecent exposure, fondling or an obscene phone call), may cause temporary emotional disturbances such as embarrassment, fear, confusion, guilt, anxiety, and a distrust of adults or strangers.

More severe incidents of sexual abuse, such as incest, rape, sodomy, exposure to pornographic activity or other forms of sexual violence may have a lasting effect on the child. Behavioral problems may include withdrawal, difficulty at school, aggression, running away, nightmares, and extreme anxiety or depression. In some cases symptoms of childhood sexual abuse may not appear until adulthood.

The month of April is considered as sexual abuse month. During this time of sexual awareness and abuse at the church, there are times that I would want to tell my testimony that it happens to young men but I refuse because of the shame that I thought it would bring on me and my family. Sometimes I often joke to myself that she probably played a very intricate part in my life preventing me from becoming gay or having homosexual tendencies. Sometimes young men growing up with predominantly female siblings usually adapt to the feminine characteristics of the household. Many times they become confused with their gender and think that it's their genetic makeup. I choose not to agree with that philosophy because God does not make mistakes. God created man and woman. Now, what I do think may have happened could be due to the chemical exposure and scientific breakthroughs in our food processing plants and scientific institutions to create faster growing fruits, vegetables, poultry, pork, and beef. These products have been chemically altered to produce mass quantities in a short period of time. I don't think enough tests have been done to see how these chemically induced products affect the ecosystem and the natural body when ingested by animals and consumed by humans. Yes we see the end product, but we do not see what happened with much of the experimentations that took place to reach that product. What happened to the results of the many documentations of the experimental animals and the effects that were produced before the food and drug administration, agricultural associations, or the environmental protection agency deemed it necessary to approve these processes? In my opinion I feel as though this has caused many defects in childbirths, child development, and altered the genetics in the male and female chromosomes. In continuation, therefore; my reason for not discussing this with anyone is that I felt as though people would laugh or criticize me if they knew that I had been abused as a child. I guess my other sisters never knew why we would fight so much. We fought like cats and dogs. As I thought about it, I wouldn't allow her to have

THE BIG MOVE

In 1977, my mother was asked by my uncle Jimbo to come to Florida to live with him. He told her that she could find a job and things would be better for us. In an attempt to get away from the Impoverished lifestyle of living in Georgia, my mother made several visits to Pompano Beach Florida. During her visits, she found things to be a little bit better than what it was in Georgia. She saw an opportunity where she could be in a position to provide more for her children. When my mother returned from her last visit, she told us about the many opportunities that were available for her and us as a family. The only problem that we had was getting there and finding a place to live. Mama had some decisions to make. She could not make the transition with all the children. My older sisters had to remain in Georgia until mama had a place large enough for them to stay. During the summer, my uncle came to Georgia and picked up my mother, myself, and my younger sisters. We didn't even pack any clothes because we were told that we would get clothes once we arrived in Florida. We arrived in Pompano Beach Florida in June of 1977. It was very hot.

The transition to our new home took some time. I found out that living in Pompano Beach Florida was at a faster pace than living in the countryside of Southeast Georgia. At the age of fourteen, I was not allowed to go anywhere by myself. I had to be in the house before it got dark. Because of my disposition of getting into fights, I was told that guys didn't fight with fists like they did in Georgia. I was very reluctant not to start any fights once we got settled. Later, I met some young men that lived on my street. We became good friends and schoolmates. The two of them would come by the house everyday to hang out or play ball. One of them would always pretend to be a preacher and proceed to lay hands on me. He would always put his hands on my forehead and command Satan to come out. He always did it in what I thought was a jokingly manner, but I wasn't too thrilled about it. I didn't like what he was doing, but I never told him. Sometimes they would come by the house looking for me, but I wouldn't answer the door. I could hear them outside calling my name. I did not want to hurt their feelings because I didn't want to associate with them when they were talking about God and Jesus Christ. I wanted to have my fun and not be tied down with going to church. We became such close friends, that the three of us even went to our senior prom together. For four years I would make every effort to avoid them when I possibly could. I enjoyed their friendship, but there were times when I just didn't want to listen to their theology about Jesus Christ. Where I came from in Georgia, we were not accustomed to having church every day and every Sunday. I was trying to adapt to the social changes of living in what I thought as a big city. After graduation, we went our separate ways. I did not see them again until some years later. The two young men that I went to high school with are now ministers of the Gospel. The one that would lay hands on you is now serving as a pastor of a well established church in the community. It is ironic how the three of us were so close in school, and once we reunited, we found out that all three of us are now servants of God.

One thing that I noticed while adjusting to my new state was my friends and other young men in the community ability to play sports. While living in Georgia, there were rare occasions that I saw someone in person actually playing basketball or football. During my freshman year in high school, I didn't know much about organized sports. There were some other friends that encouraged me to get involved in sports. All I knew how to do was run. I was very fast. I was told that I had raw natural talent and that I should consider participating in school sports. Every day after school, me and my friends would go to the park and play basketball. When it was time to choose players to play a game, I was not chosen. I would usually stand on the sideline and watch as they played. They convinced me to come on the court and try it. It was hilarious at first, but eventually I got the hang of it. I began to perfect my game until I became a better player than them. We would also go to the football field and watch the little league practices. I became so fascinated about sports that I dedicated all my evenings to learning how to play the games. During my sophomore year in high school, I was asked to come out and play football. I thought I was good enough to play varsity, so I tried out for the varsity football team. The coach told me to come even though I had not received any of my football equipment. He would always tell me that he would give me my equipment the next day. I was so determined to play varsity football that I would attend every practice without any equipment. I attended practices for two weeks before I finally quit. In my junior year, the junior varsity coach asked me to come out and play for him. I was an instant starter. I played multiple positions on offense and defense. My main position was halfback, and fullback. I was so fast, that I would always outrun many of the plays. But, I was still trying to learn the game. I remember one day in practice, the coach told me the play that was going to be executed. He told me to go out and hold my man. Once the play began, I ran to the position that was given and wrapped my arms around the opposing defensive player and threw him to the ground. The coach told me that was the right play, but he didn't mean that kind of a hold. If that was done in a game we would have been penalized fifteen yards for holding. He explained to me how to block and make tackles. From that day on my days of playing football improved. It improved so much that I was moved up to the varsity team before the season was over. After making the move to varsity, my position changed. I became a one position player. I was still a starter, but it was in a position that I didn't like. I was switched to an offensive tackle. In this position I couldn't use my speed like I wanted too. On plays where I had to pull, many times I would overrun the play. I often thought that this move hindered my chances of being noticed by many of the college scouts. I also improved in the game of basketball. I tried out for the varsity team for three years in a row. Each year, I was cut at the last cut and was only allowed to play on the Junior varsity basketball team. There were some guys on the team that I knew that I could beat at the game any day. I think it was more of favoritism than putting your skills on the court. As I walked around the school campus and in the community, I would hear other young men saying how much they wanted to be like me. I was told that I was a good athlete, but I never knew that I excelled that well. Can you imagine someone wanting to be just like you! I was a role model and didn't even know it. The problem with that was, they only knew about what I did as a football player. If they really knew me, I think they might have had second thoughts of wanting to be like me.

One of the coaches made a confession to me in 2009. Every time he would see me at a function, he would tell everyone that I was one of his best football players. He would tell them that I was the fastest on the team. That is something that I already knew. Then one day, he told me that he had a confession to make. He said that he had to get this off of his chest. He told me that the team needed some offensive lineman, and one of the other coaches suggested me. I guess it had been bothering him for some twenty seven years. He said that it was not his choice. He regretted the move, but there was nothing he could do about it. Nevertheless, I did manage to go to college. My freshman year in sports was not very productive, but I was invited to come back the following year and compete for a position on the team. My invitation to come back was based on my performance in the Crimson and Gold game at Tuskegee University. I was playing free safety and strong safety on defense. When the coach put me in I was credited for making three solo tackles, two knock downs, and one interception. The knocked down passes could have been interceptions. I heard the coach scream at me from the sidelines asking me why I didn't make the interceptions. The interception that I made was almost run back for a touchdown but one of the offensive players clothesline me before I got to the end zone.

During my individual meeting with the head coach, he explained to me where my position was on the team, and what he was proposing. He explained to me that I looked pretty good during the jamboree and had the capabilities of making the team upon returning for the Fall semester. He told me that he was recruiting two wide receivers and there was the possibility of me competing for the position. He later told me to hang out with him for the remainder of the school year so that he can give me some guidance. Evidently, I did not return to school after my freshman year. I had some major setbacks in my life that only God could see me through them. I believe without a shadow of a doubt that God had surrounded me with many angels with different assignments to help me through this journey that has been predestined for my life.

WHAT IS AN ANGEL?

Angels is considered in some religions as heavenly beings who act as a messenger of God. The Greek word for angel is (Angelos) which means messenger. The word angel is listed in the Bible over two hundred times. According to the Strong's Concordance, the word angels appear ninety three times, and the word angel's appears two times. Although we have never seen an angel, artists have pictured them appearing as babes, toddlers, and adults. Some angels are described in the Bible as possessing wings and are able to fly. We all have angels that are around us every day. Even as we sleep angels are all around us to protect us. There are good angels and there are bad angels. Lucifer who is also known as Satan was one of the heavenly angels that turned bad. He was in charge of the angelical choir. He thought that he was equal to God, and wanted to take over Gods thrown. There was a great fight and Lucifer was cast out of heaven down to earth along with a third of the angels that were supporting him. Angels are considered to be spiritual beings that sometimes take on a human form. One example can be found *in Luke 24:4-6.*

And it came to pass, as they were much perplexed thereabout, behold, two men stood by them in shining garments. And as they were afraid, and bowed down their faces to the earth, they said unto them, Why seek ye the living among the dead? He is not here, but is risen: remember how He spake unto you when He was yet in Galilee.

These two men were actually angels telling them not to be afraid and to remember the words that Jesus had told them.

Angels can also appear to us in a vision just like they did with Mary the mother of Jesus. Gabriel was sent by God to tell her of the miraculous conception that would take place in her.

Luke 1:26-38 *And in the sixth month the angel Gabriel was sent from God unto a city of Galilee, named Nazareth, To a virgin espoused to a man whose name was Joseph, of the house of David; and the virgin's name was Mary. And the angel came in unto her, and said, Hail, thou that art highly favoured, the Lord is with thee: blessed art thou among women. And when she saw him, she was troubled at his saying, and cast in her mind what manner of salutation this should be. And the angel said unto her, Fear not, Mary: for thou hast found favour with God. And, behold, thou shalt conceive in thy womb, and bring forth a son, and shalt call his name Jesus. He shall be great, and shall be called the Son of the Highest: and the Lord God shall give unto him the throne of his father David: And he shall reign over the house of Jacob for ever; and of his kingdom there shall be no end. Then said Mary unto the angel, How shall this be, seeing I know not a man? And the angel answered and said unto her, The Holy Ghost shall come upon thee, and the power of the Highest shall overshadow thee: therefore also that holy thing which shall be born of thee shall be called the Son of God. And, behold, thy cousin Elisabeth, she hath also conceived a son in her old age: and this is the sixth month with her, who was called barren. For with God nothing shall be impossible. And Mary said, Behold the handmaid of the Lord; be it unto me according to thy word. And the angel departed from her.*

The angel also gave confirmation to Joseph concerning the birth of Jesus Christ.

Matthew 1:20 *But while he thought on these things, behold, the angel of the Lord appeared unto him in a dream, saying, Joseph, thou son of David, fear not to take unto thee Mary thy wife: for that which is conceived in her is of the Holy Ghost.*

There are many other instances of where angels have appeared by vision or in person to give Gods people a message. Angels are also helpers and encouragers.

John 5:4 For an angel went down at a certain season into the pool, and troubled the water: whosoever then first after the troubling of the water stepped in was made whole of whatsoever disease he had.

The bible tells us that Jesus also was ministered to by an angel when he went into the garden of Gethsemane to pray. In Luke 22:40-43 it gives us a clear example of how angels are destined to show up and minister to us by strengthening us and encouraging us.

And when he was at the place, he said unto them, Pray that ye enter not into temptation. And he was withdrawn from them about a stone's cast, and kneeled down, and prayed, Saying, Father, if thou be willing, remove this cup from me: nevertheless not my will, but thine, be done. And there appeared an angel unto him from heaven, strengthening him.

Even when he was in the wilderness for forty days, there were angels there to minister to him. *Mark 1:13 And he was there in the wilderness forty days, tempted of Satan; and was with the wild beasts; and the angels ministered unto him*

In Isaiah 6:1-2 angels are depicted as heavenly beings praising and worshiping the Lord. In the year that king Uzziah died I saw also the Lord sitting upon a throne, high and lifted up, and his train filled the temple. Above it stood the seraphim's: each one had six wings; with twain he covered his face, and with twain he covered his feet, and with twain he did fly. And one cried unto another, and said, Holy, holy, holy, is the Lord of hosts: the whole earth is full of his glory.

Just like there are angels sent by God, Satan has his demonic angels as well. The difference is that Satan and his angels go before God accusing us to God. His case against us is, if we love God so much; why do we constantly do the things that we do. It seems as though he constantly tells God to look at his creation. These are the ones that you created in the likeness of your image. I don't think you will find one righteous person among them. They say that they love you, but will not keep any of your commandments. He doesn't realize that we have an advocate in Jesus Christ. When we commit a sin, we can rest assure that when we go before God and confess our sins that he is faithful and just to forgive us and cleanse us of all unrighteousness. Therefore, Satan and his angels were cast out of heaven down to earth.

Rev. 12:7-10 And there was war in heaven: Michael and his angels fought against the dragon; and the dragon fought and his angels, And prevailed not; neither was their place found any more in heaven. And the great dragon was cast out, that old serpent, called the Devil, and Satan, which deceiveth the whole world: he was cast out into the earth, and his angels were cast out with him. And I heard a loud voice saying in heaven, Now is come salvation, and strength, and the kingdom of our God, and the power of his Christ: for the accuser of our brethren is cast down, which accused them before our God day and night.

We have to be careful of who we are trusting and what we are trusting. We have to keep an open mind to the things that we engage in. Satan and his angels are deceptive, manipulating, and destructive. He is like a roaring lion seeking whom he may devour. 1 Peter 5:8 Be sober, be vigilant; because your adversary the devil, as a roaring lion, walketh about, seeking whom he may devour: Satin appeared before God twice to get his permission to attack Job. This lets us know that Satin cannot do anything to us unless God allows it to happen. The first time Satan appeared before God was in Job 1:6-7.

Now there was a day when the sons of God came to present themselves before the Lord, and Satan came also among them. And the Lord said unto Satan, Whence comest thou? Then Satan answered the Lord, and said, From going to and fro in the earth, and from walking up and down in it. Job 1:8 And the Lord said unto Satan, Hast thou considered my servant Job, that there is none like him in the earth, a perfect and an upright man, one that feareth God, and escheweth evil?

The second time Satan appeared was in Job 2:2.

And the Lord said unto Satan, From whence comest thou? And Satan answered the Lord, and said, From going to and fro in the earth, and from walking up and down in it. Job 2:3 And the Lord said unto Satan, Hast thou considered my servant Job, that there is none like him in the earth, a perfect and an upright man, one that feareth God, and escheweth evil? and still he holdeth fast his integrity, although thou movedst me against him, to destroy him without cause.

We as children of God must understand that our adversary is out to destroy us. We must hold fast to that which we believe. We must keep the faith. We must maintain our integrity even when the walls seem like they are caving in on us. We must stay away from evil.

1 Thes. 5:22 (KJV) says Abstain from all appearance of evil. Anything that seems evil or no good, stay away from it. Arm yourself with the armor of God. We must put on the whole armor of God so that we can withstand the wiles of the devil.

Ephes. 6:10-18 Finally, my brethren, be strong in the Lord, and in the power of his might. Put on the whole armour of God, that ye may be able to stand against the wiles of the devil. For we wrestle not against flesh and blood, but against principalities, against powers, against the rulers of the darkness of this world, against spiritual wickedness in high places. Wherefore take unto you the whole armour of God, that ye may be able to withstand in the evil day, and having done all, to stand. Stand therefore, having your loins girt about with truth, and having on the breastplate of righteousness; And your feet shod with the preparation of the gospel of peace; Above all, taking the shield of faith, wherewith ye shall be able to quench all the fiery darts of the wicked. And take the helmet of salvation, and the sword of the Spirit, which is the word of God: Praying always with all prayer and supplication in the Spirit, and watching thereunto with all perseverance and supplication for all saints; nowing that one day, Jesus is coming back.

When Jesus returns on judgment day, he will return along with his holy angels to judge the world. That's why God said, as I paraphrase," Let the wheat and the tare grow together and on the Day of Judgment, I would do the separating". One day we all will have to stand before Christ and give an account of everything that we have done in this body while living here on earth. What will our response be?

Matthew 25:41-46 Then shall he say also unto them on the left hand, Depart from me, ye cursed, into everlasting fire, prepared for the devil and his angels: For I was an hungred, and ye gave me no meat: I was thirsty, and ye gave me no drink: I was a stranger, and ye took me not in: naked, and ye clothed me not: sick, and in prison, and ye visited me not. Then shall they also answer him, saying, Lord, when saw we thee an hungred, or athirst, or a stranger, or naked, or sick, or in prison, and did not minister unto thee? Then shall he answer them, saying, Verily I say unto you, Inasmuch as ye did it not to one of the least of these, ye did it not to me. And these shall go away into everlasting punishment: but the righteous into life eternal.

One of the most comforting things that I love about being a Christian is that there are angels that rejoice when a non-believer gives their life to Christ. To keep it simple, turn from their wicked ways and live according to the Word of God by accepting the teachings of Jesus Christ and making them permanent in their lives. Jesus uses three examples to show us how we rejoice when we lose something that we cherish so dearly. He shows us what happens when we find it, or when it returns to us. He uses a lost sheep, a coin, and a child.

Luke 15:4-10 What man of you, having an hundred sheep, if he lose one of them, doth not leave the ninety and nine in the wilderness, and go after that which is lost, until he find it? And when he hath found it, he layeth it on his shoulders, rejoicing. And when he cometh home, he calleth together his friends and neighbours, saying unto them, Rejoice with me; for I have found my sheep which was lost. I say unto you, that likewise joy shall be in heaven over one sinner that repenteth, more than over ninety and nine just persons, which need no repentance. Either what woman having ten pieces of silver, if she lose one piece, doth not light a candle, and sweep the house, and seek diligently till she find it? And when she hath found it, she calleth her friends and her neighbours together, saying, Rejoice with me; for I have found the piece which I had lost. Likewise, I say unto you, there is joy in the presence of the angels of God over one sinner that repenteth.

In the case of the prodigal son, after he regained his senses, he realized his mistakes. He repented and returned home to his father. That's the same thing God expects from us. He wants us to repent and to return to him. Luke 15:21-24

And the son said unto him, Father, I have sinned against heaven, and in thy sight, and am no more worthy to be called thy son. But the father said to his servants, Bring forth the best robe, and put it on him; and put a ring on his hand, and shoes on his feet: And bring hither the fatted calf, and kill it; and let us eat, and be merry: For this my son was dead, and is alive again; he was lost, and is found. And they began to be merry.

I am more convinced now than ever that there are angels that walk amongst us today. Some angels are messengers. Some angels are guardians or protectors, and some are ministers or servers. I am not sure if I could consider myself as an angel, but I do think that I have some angelical characteristics. Whether I dream dreams or have visions, I believe that they all exist.

THE DISTINCT CALL

When I was a little boy about eight years old, I almost got hit by a passing car. One day I was playing in the yard near the road imagining that I was an airplane. I would stretch out my arms as if I had wings, lower my head and pretend to fly. This was my first encounter of wanting to fly or being fascinated about flying. So I ran out into the road with my arms extended and my head held down right in front of a passing car. Immediately I banked to the right as the car was approaching and ran or should I say flew back into the yard. I noticed that move from watching the crop dusters as they flew over the house for so many times. Up until this day my uncle Robert continues to tease me concerning this incident. Since then, I have always been fascinated about airplanes and birds in flight. Even today, every once and a while, I would take my binoculars and search the sky for whatever bird that I can find to get a closer look at them. Although I've always pretended to fly since I was eight, I believe that my dreams of flying started when I was around twelve years old.

One of the things that I would do to past the time was to lie down in the grassy fields near my house. I would look up into the sky and wonder what it would be like to have wings like a bird and fly. I would focus my mind and see if I could levitate off the ground. This became one of my favorite things to do to pass the time.

Another favorite past time was exploring the wooded areas around my house. One day I had an unusual experience while I was on one of my adventures in the woods. When I explained what happened to my mother, she did not believe me. I was told by an old pioneer in the community that I had a divine visit from God. It all began in a little town in Georgia named Vidette. We lived out in the countryside. The nearest largest city was about fifty miles away. There wasn't that many houses near ours and no young boys my age to play with. I spent most of my time playing with my dog Ringo. Ringo was the kind of dog that would not let anyone approach near me including my sisters. Many times I would command my dog to attack my sisters. My dog and I enjoyed exploring the wooded areas surrounding our house. I would run through the woods and climb trees while Ringo would wait for me from beneath. One day while I was playing in the woods, I began to climb a tree. I heard this voice call my name. No one knew where I was and what I was doing so I ignored the voice and continued to climb the tree. All of a sudden I heard the voice again. At this point I had begun to get afraid because Ringo was my watchdog and he was not barking. All I could see him doing was standing underneath the tree wagging his tail. I continued to play in the tree, and then I heard the voice again.

The Bible says in Hebrew 4: 7," To-day if ye shall hear his voice, harden not your hearts." In John 10:27-28 says, My sheep hear my voice, and I know them, and they follow me: And I give unto them eternal life; and they shall never perish, neither shall any man pluck them out of my hand.

I realized that this voice was unusual. It was like no other voice that I had heard before. After hearing the voice the third time, I became terrified. I hurried down the tree and began to run home as fast as I could. Ringo was right behind me. When I reached home, I told my momma that I had heard someone call my name in the woods. I told her that it did not sound like someone's voice that I had heard before. I asked her what was going on and she replied," Get away from me. You don't know what you are talking about. You didn't hear any such voice. Later, I went to visit this little old lady by the name of Ms. Mozelle Sprout. She lived less than a mile from where I lived. She always fed me when I came to visit her because she thought that I was hungry. I explained to her what I had encountered in the woods. She began to explain to me what had occurred. It was brief and unexpected. She told me that now I have two sets of eyes. She said "You now have an inward set of eyes and you have an outward set of eyes. You may not understand it now, but you will when you get older." I felt a sigh of relief and continued to eat. When it came to spiritual things, I was very naive. I didn't go to church that often, because the pastor of the church pastored more than one church. We had to wait until the Sunday that he would preach at our church to worship and praise God. I can recall every year when we would attend a church revival. I was always excited and eager to get to the church. I guess it was because of the gathering of many families that would bring their children. Every year I would watch as some of the children would approach the altar when an invitation was extended for salvation and membership. I would watch the evangelist as he would whisper something in each child's ear. Upon the correct response, he would continue to give the new converts instructions pertaining to who their deacon would be, church membership and baptism. I could hardly wait until my time came. Finally it happened, I can recall one winter revival giving my hand to the preacher only because my mother told me that it was my time. I didn't understand what I was doing. I was only following her instructions. She even told me what to say if the preacher asked me some questions. I remember repeating some words after the preacher. I guess that was considered accepting Jesus Christ. This was the beginning of my spiritualistic part of growing up. There were still those alternating Sundays in which the pastor would preach at our church.

Every second Saturday of each month, people from miles around would come to the society hall. Every family from the surrounding community would come and pay their society dues. These funds were used to help those that were in need. Many would bring homemade cakes, their favorite dishes, collard greens, southern fried chicken, and make some good old fashioned lemonade.

Before we could have anything to eat, we would always have a devotional program. Ms Mozelle would always have little speeches for me to do. I guess this was one way of preparing me for what was to come later in life. It was nearly ten years later when I actually began to listen to the voice of God. In the mean

THE DREAMS

One night on February 4, 2009 as I was sleeping, early during that morning I had a dream. The dream was so real and intense as though it was actually happening at that particular moment. What awakened me was a voice in the dream telling me to record the dream in detail. When I regained my senses, I asked myself, was this real or was I just dreaming. The next night it happened again. This time the voice told me to record all my dreams for the remaining of the month. Every morning between the hours of 3 o'clock and 4 o'clock I would wake up and began recording the dream or dreams that I dreamt. I didn't hesitate to begin writing down each dream in detail. In the compilation of dreams that I recorded, they were about running, flying, and preaching. I am not an expert on interpreting dreams, but I would like to explain what these three types of dreams mean to me.

According to Frank and Ida Mae Hammond, in their book; Pigs in the Parlor, in chapter 23 The final conflict; they wrote. "Throughout Biblical history, God on occasion spoke to His servants through visions and dreams. On the day of Pentecost, Peter quoted from the prophet Joel: Acts 2:17

And it shall come to pass in the last days, saith God; I will pour out of my Spirit upon all flesh: and your sons and your daughters shall prophesy, and your young men shall see visions, and your old men shall dream dreams.

As I read the beginning of chapter 23 in the book titled "Pigs in the Parlor", I had that same feeling that the Lord wanted me to minister to someone through my dreams. Not only did I have these spiritual dreams, but God gave me the ability to interpret those dreams. I again take this quote from Frank and Ida Mae Hammond.

"A spiritual dream cannot be figured out, it must be interpreted." This is my interpretation of the three types of dreams that the Spirit has given me. My interpretation of my dreams of running can be interpreted as; being diligent because the race is not given to the swift, but to the one that endures to the end.

1 Cor. 9:24 Know ye not that they which run in a race run all, but one receiveth the prize? So run, that ye may obtain.

Hebrews 12:1 Wherefore seeing we also are compassed about with so great a cloud of witnesses, let us lay aside every weight, and the sin which doth so easily beset us, and let us run with patience the race that is set before us.

The way I see it is, that we must stay the course. We must run the race that is given to us. I cannot run someone else's race. I cannot run a marathon when I am a sprinter. I must learn how to stay in my lane. I cannot run a race with excess baggage. I cannot run a race with distractions. When I run, I must run to obtain a prize. I must stay focused. I must run like a race horse with blinders on. The blinders are used to block them from looking at the opposing runner adjacent to him. There are so many witnesses that have run before me. I can hear them in the stands cheering me on. As I take another quote from the Hammonds,

"They were all the Christians who ever lived and were now looking down upon the world from their heavenly position. All of the patriarchs and saints of the Old and New Testament eras were in the stands. There were Abraham, Jacob, Isaac, Josheph, David, Daniel, Jeremiah, Isaiah, Peter, James and John and all the rest. They were looking with keenest of anticipation to see how those of us in this generation would do." Therefore, I can't let doubt and fear keep me from reaching the finish line. If I do allow this to happen, my running would be in vain.

To dream of preaching means: Be steadfast unmovable always abounding in the work of God.

1Cor. 15:58 Therefore, my beloved brethren, be ye stedfast, unmovable, always abounding in the work of the Lord forasmuch as ye know that your labour is not in vain in the Lord.

There are three things that I want to convey. The first thing is to be steadfast. We must hold on to the Gospel of Jesus Christ that has been preached into our souls. Secondly, we must be unmovable knowing that when Christ comes back we are going to be changed. We will be changed from corruptible to incorruptible. We will be changed from mortal to immortality. We must be like a tree planted by the rivers of water. We must meditate on his word day and night. We must become saturated in the word of God. The word of God must permeate throughout our lives. Thirdly, we must abound in the work of the Lord. We must do the work of the Lord. Go ye therefore in all nations baptizing in the name of the Father, the Son, and Holy Spirit. We must be about our Fathers business.

My dreams of flying can be interpreted as; be patient wait upon the Lord.

Isaiah 40:31 But they that wait upon the Lord shall renew their strength; they shall mount up with wings as eagles; they shall run, and not be weary; and they shall walk, and not faint.

When we find ourselves getting weary, God will refresh us or renew our strength. He will give us the strength to soar above those difficult moments. An old eagle never feels like he's old because he is regenerated when he produces new feathers. With these new feathers, he feels like a young eagle. This is what allows him to live a long productive cycle. We must be like eagles.

not watch that event because I fell asleep before it happened. During that time while I was sleeping, I dreamed that I was running along with Michael while he was competing. When Michael pulled up lame coming down the stretch, in my dream I also pulled up lame. When I woke up, I had injured my left ankle. I think Michael had pulled his left groin. I got up favoring my left leg. My wife asked me what was wrong with my leg. I told her that I had injured it in my dream while competing with Michael Johnson. My wife laughed at me and told me not to tell anyone about that dream. I guess I fulfilled my dream of running in an Olympic event.

One of the most hilarious dreams that I could remember having was during my senior year in high school. During my senior year at Blanche Ely High School, one day I decided to goof off. One day while I was in my accounting class, I decided to sit in the back of the class and go to sleep. During the time that I was sleeping, I began to dream of playing football. In my dream, I was a wide receiver playing professionally in the NFL. We were playing the Oakland Raiders on this particular game day. Oakland had this great cornerback by the name of Lester Hayes. He was a hard hitting, great coverage corner. He was well known for wearing an excessive amount of stickem on his hands and socks. Sometimes he also liked to play dirty by getting in some cheap shots after the play was over. As the game went on, I ran a crossing route and the ball was thrown to me. I made the catch and Lester made the tackle. As I was getting up, Lester kicked me and got away with it. I told him when I got up that the next time we run that play and if he makes the tackle that I was going to kick him back. Low and behold a few plays later, we ran the same play again. I made the catch, and Lester made the tackle. As we were getting up, I kindly reminded him about when he kicked me on one of the previous plays. I ended up giving him a swift kick. In reality, I kicked over the desk that was in front of me while I was sleeping in class. The most embarrassing thing was that the teacher asked me what was I doing, and I immediately told her that I was dreaming. She asked me to tell the entire class what I was dreaming about. For weeks I was the talk of the class. From that point, I tried my best not to fall asleep in the classroom again. I had always dreamed of playing in the NFL. To me, this was as close as I would ever get. Not only that, but, the Oakland Raiders became my favorite football team to watch.

ENCOURAGED BY AN ANGEL

After graduating from Blanche Ely high school in 1981, I attended Tuskegee University in Tuskegee Alabama. I was part of 100 freshmen from across the country that was enrolled in the upward bound summer program. We only had three courses to take during the summer session. One of those courses was freshmen orientation. This course was designed to help us get acquainted with the campus as-well-as adjust to the college atmosphere. When the fall semester started, I was already familiar with the campus and its surroundings.

One day I went to the admissions building to ask for some information. A counselor by the name of Mrs. Shirley W. Curry took my information. As we were talking, she told me of a young man from Fort Lauderdale Fl by the name of Darryl Beasley. He was an assistant to the dorm director. She told me to get to know him. When I met him, immediately he began to call me his little brother. Little did I know that he was an ordained minister! He encouraged me to go to the campus chapel every Sunday. Throughout my freshman year of college, he looked out for me whenever I found myself in need. He would cook home cooked meals and invite many of the students that were there over to eat. He was very influential in helping me to get back on track when I was failing. He was also my way to get back and forth to Florida whenever we had a holiday or a long weekend. This is one of the reasons that I believe angels have been with me every since I was born.

I can recall another incident where I and some dorm mates we were indulging with drugs and alcohol. Only God could have placed his angels there to watch over me. Everybody in the room was getting wasted. For some reason no matter how much I indulged in it, I could not get high or get a buzz. The room was filled with smoke. Everybody was laid out on the beds and the floor. Even though we had towels under the door and around the windows, you could still smell the odor. We were alerted that the campus security was on their way. Since I was the one that was aware of what was going on, I managed to help my roommate and some others to get out of the room before security got there. I think this was one of God's ways of letting me know that this wasn't the way he wanted me go.

Unfortunately some things happened that I had no idea would happened. I did not play football my freshmen year. When I arrived at Tuskegee, I reported to coach Schizom office. He told me that I was two weeks late and that he was no longer the head coach because he had retired. He told me that if I wanted to play, that I had to talk with the present head coach. Coach Bullie told me to come to tryouts during the spring training sessions. During the spring practices, I ran and went to weight training until it was time for the Crimson and Gold game. Prior to leaving for the summer, I had left a big impression on the head football coach Alonzo Bullie. The good news was that he invited me back for the next season to compete for a position on the football team as a wide receiver. The coach said because I had good hands and was very fast; he thought that I had a very good chance of beating out the new recruits for a position. Also, the young lady that I was dating got pregnant and would have nothing else to do with me. She told me what she was going to do and there was nothing I could do about it. I told her that I would stay home and get a job to take care of her and the baby. We left Tuskegee for the summer. Diana gave birth to a baby boy named Adrian Emanuel on April 21, 1982. Upon returning for the fall semester of 1982, I received a letter from the school stating that all upper classmen would have to move out of the dorms because of the large numbers of incoming freshmen. I tried reluctantly to find a place to stay but without travail. My sister who was a previous student at Tuskegee told me to go to Dorothy Hall and see if I could stay there until I was able to find a place to stay for the semester. After spending a week in Dorothy Hall guest rooms with no more money, I decided to return home. After returning home, I sent many letters to. Diana's old dorm hoping that someone would give them to her. The letters never came back to me so I assumed that she got them. After a while, I stopped writing letters. These two ordeals were so devastating to me. I came from a poor family that was giving me little or no support. I was actually relying on financial aid and making the football team to remain in school. Not only that, I was looking forward to seeing someone that I had cared about and wanted to give up a college career to be with her and our son.

Once I returned home, I was unable to find a job. Every day I sat around the house doing nothing but eating, watching television, and sleeping. I was so depressed that I didn't even want to look for a job. There were some days in which I would go to my old high school football field and run around the track. I would run as though I was a mad man. While I was running, I would he crying and singing. The song that I would sing was The Commodores "Jesus is love" by lead vocalist Lionel Richie. This was my consolation that God was with me. Whenever I would feel down and out, I would find a solitary place where I could just sing me a song. As Lionel would say, "Father help your children. Don't let them fall by the side of the road. Teach them to love one another that heaven might find a place in their heart. Jesus is love he want let you down." That song was so comforting to me. Not only did it bring tears to my eyes, but it also lifted me out of my moment of despair.

One day my mother and I got into a heated argument. She said some things to me that really upset me. She asked one question that really ticked me off. She asked," What are you going to do if you get a girlfriend and want to take her out on a date? I told her that I would ask her for the money. She said, "I am tired of giving you money." Then she said, "I don't care where you get a job, as long as you get out of here." She said you can get a job pumping gas at the gas station for all I care." I was so angry at her, that I got up and left the house in tears. I told her that I was not going to get a job. I told her that all I wanted to do was walk the streets and become a bum. A few minutes later as I was walking down the street, an unknown man drove by and asked me was I working. I told him no. He asked me if I wanted to make forty dollars unloading trash off of his truck. I told him yes and proceeded to get into his truck. I had never seen this man in my entire life. He could have been a murderer, a rapist, or even a child molester. The strange thing about it was, as we began to leave my neighborhood he kept asking me this question. "What are you going to do with your life?" Then he took me about ten miles to an undeveloped area of the county near the everglades. There were no homes, just canals and swamps. There he left me and the truck and said he would return later when he thinks that I have finished unloading the truck. After I had unloaded the truck, he returned just as he said. In the meantime, during the return trip home, he asked me the question again. I don't remember the exact response that I gave him, but I do remember saying something to the effect that I was going to return to college. As we were heading back to my house, there was not a word said. It was totally quiet. When we reached my house I got out of the truck. He paid me the money that we had agreed upon and I never saw him again. I went into the house and told my mother what had happened. Without a shadow of a doubt, I believe that this was my angel that was assigned to me for that particular moment in my life. The scripture is true about what it says about strangers in the book of Hebrews.

Hebrews 13:2. (KJV) Be not forgetful to entertain strangers: for thereby some have entertained angels unawares.

I don't suggest that to every young person, because we teach them to be aware of strangers. During my time of depression, God had sent an angel to minister to me because I literally wanted to give up on my future and my life. I had no hope, and I had lost all faith.

After that encounter, I was so excited for the rest of that day. I think this was the turning point of my life. From that point on,

I went to work wherever I could get a job to save money to go back to college. I went to work as a day labor for a deacon of a local church. Every morning we would meet in the office to get our job assignments and after that he would pray for our safety on the job and a safe return home. Sometimes I would have the opportunity to ride with his son. He would often tell me about how he went to school at Lane University and that I should go back to school. I assured him that I was going to go back to college.

During my brief stay at home, I went and signed up for the Air force. I guess it was because of my love for flying. I was scheduled to take an entrance exam before I could take my physical. So, I took the entrance exam. When the results of the exam came back, I overheard the recruiters talking about my results. I was not sure of what had happened. They told me that they wanted me to retake the exam. My initial thought was that they thought that I had probably cheated on the exam. As stubborn as I was, I never went back to retake the exam. In August of 1983, I registered to go to a local trade school. I attended Ft. Lauderdale School of Allied Health Careers for two years studying to become a Medical Laboratory Technician. After completing all of my course requirements, I selected not to do my externship. Instead, immediately I prepared myself to go back to Tuskegee University for the fall semester in 1985. Upon my return to Tuskegee, I had a new focus on life and a new determination to succeed. My grades improved to the point where I was taken off of academic probation. My grade point average increased from a 1.75 to a 3.00 on a 4.0 scale. I maintained that GPA the remaining of my terms at Tuskegee. I was placed in the honors dorm and had excellent roommates. I even saw a few of my original classmates that were there when I was a freshman. One of the most important things was an old friend of the young lady that I dated was still there. She asked me had I been keeping in touch with her and my son. I told her no, but I also explained to her that I tried and that I sent many letters but received no answer. The letters were sent to White Hall, but were never returned to me. I assumed that she got the letters but just didn't want to respond to me. She then began to show me a picture of the child. He looked just like me. That was her only picture so she kept it. I had hoped that she would contact her and let her know that I was back in school. I resumed my education at Tuskegee University until the Spring of 1987.

In 1987, I found myself experiencing more anxiety and disappointments. I received a call from my mother saying that she needed me to come home and take care of her. I thought that I would only be home for one semester. My mother's health declined so I stayed at home longer than I intended to stay. Although I was a little disappointed, this time I was able to get a job earning a decent wage. After that, everything seemed to be going great. I had money, I had my own apartment, and I was able to get me a nice car. To me, I was living the good life. I also met a young lady that had tried to talk to me when I was in high school. At the time, she was a friend of my baby sister attending middle school. She would come over to my house to play with my sister but at the same time try to talk to me. She said that I showed no interest in her even when she would take my money and my shoes. I did everything that I could to avoid her.

As the story is told, one year I came home from college and she caught my attention. I never knew that it was the same little girl that came over to the house to talk to my sister because she had grown up. One day a friend and I made a bet to see who would get to date her first. We had a few friendly words, and that was it. I saw her again when I came home for the summer. This time she had a baby with her. A year later, as I was running past her place of employment, I heard a voice calling me. I turned around and it was her peering out of a window. I turned around and asked her was she calling me. She said yes. We talked a little bit and that was the end of the story.

It wasn't until after I returned from college that fate brought us back together. Later, we began to go out on dates. One night after we had went out on a date, I told her that I didn't love her, and that I would not be seeing her again. I left and went home. When I got home to my apartment, a voice spoke to me and told me to call her back and tell her that I do love her. I responded to the voice and gave her a call. I explained to her my actions from the previous night and told her that I loved her. I asked her for another chance. We dated for four years before we got married. I am convinced that she is another angel that God has placed in my life. In April of 1991, I was invited to come to church by Leila. She wanted me to hear this dynamic preacher. Prior to accepting the invitation, I was part of a group of guys that sat around every Sunday morning playing cards, cooking hefty meals, and drinking beer. We called ourselves Knights of the Square table. We all decided to accept the invitation of the wives and girlfriends and attend church. After hearing this preacher for this first time, there was something that had my attention. Eventually, I gave up the card games and made Sunday mornings a day of worship. I gave up the Sunday morning ritual of drinking and playing cards. I joined the church, and later got married to the woman that I loved Ms. Leila Holmes. As we know, everywhere we go it is already predestined by God. It was not by fate that I joined that particular church, but it was God that drew me there.

Instantly the moment I joined I was asked to come and help with the youth of our church serving as a youth counselor for the young men. I was also asked to teach one of the Sunday school classes. Later I was giving the task of being the president of the newly formed #2 usher board. In 1993, I received a call from the chairman of the deacon board. He told me that I was being considered as one of seven candidates for the new deacons of the church. I was asked to talk it over with my wife, pray about it and let him know if I accept. In 1994 I was ordained as a deacon of the church. As I was fulfilling my duties as a deacon, I began to receive messages from the Lord reminding me of the time when I first heard this mysterious voice when I was about twelve years old. I can vividly remember the voice telling me to read Ezekiel chapter 33. I don't ever recall reading that passage of scripture during that time. After reading the chapter it was evident that God was telling me that he wanted me to tell the people thus says the Lord.

Ezekiel 33:7-12 (KJV) So thou, O son of man, I have set thee a watchman unto the house of Israel; therefore thou shalt hear the word at my mouth, and warn them from me. When I say unto the wicked, O wicked man, thou shalt surely die; if thou dost not speak to warn the wicked from his way, that wicked man shall die in his iniquity; but his blood will I require at thine hand. Nevertheless, if thou warn the wicked of his way to turn from it; if he do not turn from his way, he shall die in his iniquity; but thou hast delivered thy soul. Therefore, O thou son of man, speak unto the house of Israel; Thus ye speak, saying, If our transgressions and our sins be upon us, and we pine away in them, how should we then live? Say unto them, As I live, saith the Lord God, I have no pleasure in the death of the wicked; but that the wicked turn from his way and live: turn ye, turn ye from your evil ways; for why will ye die, O house of Israel? Therefore, thou son of man, say unto the children of thy people, The righteousness of the righteous shall not deliver him in the day of his transgression: as for the wickedness of the wicked, he shall not fall thereby in the day that he turneth from his wickedness; neither shall the righteous be able to live for his righteousness in the day that he sinneth.

The Lord also directed me to the first chapter of Jeremiah verse 4 thru 10.

Jeremiah 1:4-10 (KJV) Then the word of the Lord came unto me, saying, Before I formed thee in the belly I knew thee; and before thou camest forth out of the womb I sanctified thee, and I ordained thee a prophet unto the nations. Then said I, Ah, Lord God! behold, I cannot speak: for I am a child. But the Lord said unto me, Say not, I am a child: for thou shalt go to all that I shall send thee, and whatsoever I command thee thou shalt speak. Be not afraid of their faces: for I am with thee to deliver thee, saith the Lord. Then the Lord put forth his hand, and touched my mouth. And the Lord said unto me, Behold, I have put my words in thy mouth. See, I have this day set thee over the nations and over the kingdoms, to root out, and to pull down, and to destroy, and to throw down, to build, and to plant.

This baffled me because I couldn't phantom myself standing in front of people talking. I took Public speaking in college and got a B in class without giving one oral presentation. Yes, I did all of my written assignments, but I was never able to stand before anyone to speak. I would always get nervous and shake very badly when I stood in front of the class.

At this point, I had an idea of what the message was, but I was still reluctant to accept my calling. I tried everything that I could do to avoid preaching the word of God. Some would say that I was running from God. I literally told God that I did not want to be in this position. It was as if I was in a tug-of-war with God and the Devil. When God will tell me one thing, the devil would tell me the opposite. I had to choose which one that I would be loyal to. The Bible says that you cannot serve God and mammon. It says either you will love the one or you will hate the other. Joshua says it this way.

Joshua 24:15 (KJV) And if it seem evil unto you to serve the Lord, choose you this day whom ye will serve; whether the gods which your fathers served that were on the other side of the flood, or the gods of the Amorites, in whose land ye dwell: but as for me and my house, we will serve the Lord.

I chose to straddle the fence. I tried to serve God and at the same time do my thing for the joy that it would bring. I had a Jonas spirit in me. Remember when God told Jonah to go down to Nineveh and he got on the boat to go to Tarshis. Because of his disobedience, He was swallowed up by a big fish until he repented and chose to do God's will. God had to show me what will happen to me if I didn't do what he asked of me I was just like a wild horse. God literally had to break me before I gave in to him. He had to break me physically, spiritually and financially. I was like a ship without a sail. I was drifting father away from God. As the saints of old would say, "I was sinking deep in sin far from a peaceful shore. I was very deeply stained within sinking to rise no more. But the Master of the sea he heard my despairing cry, and from the waters he lifted me now safe am I.

Things began to happen in my life that would wreak havoc in the lives of me and my wife. I was laid off of my job after eleven years of working for one company. There were some issues that I had been dealing with that was like a thorn in my flesh. They would not go away. My wife had threatened to leave me. At one point, she even put a knife to my throat while I was lying on the floor pretending to be asleep. It wasn't until I had almost hit rock bottom that the messenger came to me again. This time I didn't hesitate to say yes Lord. That night it seems as though I cried all night long. I lay prostrate on the floor and I yielded everything and turned it over to God. Later I told my pastor that I had been called by God to preach the gospel. He called me in his office and we talked for a few minutes. He asked me how I knew that I was being called by God. I began to tell him about the visions that I had from the prophets of the Old Testament such as; Ezekiel and Jeremiah. I told him that I kept having these visions. He told me, that he could not have a preaching deacon. He said that he would give me some time to think it over and if the spirit was still leading me in that direction, he has no other choice but to give me the chance to do my initial sermon.

After one year of seeking the Lord for direction, on January 30, 2000 I preached my first sermon titled "My cup runneth over". After accepting the destiny which God had given me, many things began to change in my life. I began to be more compassionate for the people than I had previously been. I became overwhelmed with trying to accommodate every issue that was brought to my attention. Someone made a comment during one of the church services that, "If you are in a jam, call Minister Habersham." I thought of that as a compliment to the work that God had for me to do. My assignment as a messenger of God increased. Through the leadership of my Pastor Dr. Robert C. Stanley who is led by the Holy Spirit has taught me so much in such a short time. His motto is to follow me as I follow Christ. Since 1997, I was in charge of the Hopewell Missionary Baptist Church's Outreach Ministry. Because he is my pastor, I have sought after his knowledge and wisdom concerning many things about the ministry. Most of all, I have relied completely on the Holy Spirit to lead and guide me in the ministry. Before I lead God's people in treacherous areas of the community, I always ask him for his guidance. I ask him to place his angels around us to keep us safe from all dangers seen and unseen. I ask him to protect us from all evil spirits that we may encounter as we travel from place to place. I ask him to go before us and show us those who he will have us to reach. Touch their hearts and minds that they will receive the message that you have imparted in us to give to them.

As I reminisce about the ventures that I have encountered, God was with me all the way. There have been times on this journey where I was literally guarded by the angels and led by the Holy Spirit. I can recall one night on my way home from church. I saw a long time friend whom I played basketball with many times. I picked him up and asked him where he was going. He showed me his gun and said that he wanted to kill someone. Immediately my response to him was why you would want to kill someone. That night I took a few extra minutes of my time and talked to him of the consequences that he would face if he carried out his plan. Finally he asked me to drop him off on the corner of the street. When I saw him again, he thanked me for intervening that night. He told me that what I shared with him encouraged him. To this day he and his family are doing well. Many of the children are teenagers and some have finished school. I can recall another situation where I approached an apartment where a man and woman were having an argument. As I knocked on the door, the woman told me to come in. The door was already opened, but enclosed by a screen door. The man told me not to step foot in his door otherwise he would shoot me. I saw what appeared to be a rifle and began to back away. The lady again said to me come on in he is not going to shoot he's just bluffing. At that time, I weighed about 230 pounds all muscle. I stood six feet one inches tall. My initial thought was that I am big enough to take him if he tries me. The Holy Spirit stepped in and told me to move on to the next door. I have really learned how to trust the Holy Spirit because he will not lead you in the wrong places.

Matthew 10:14 (KJV) And whosoever shall not receive you, nor hear your words, when ye depart out of that house or city, shake off the dust of your feet.

This lets me know that God even protects us while doing the ministry that he has allowed us to do.

There are many other instances where the Lord has dealt with my heart concerning people that have been broken hearted, outcast, down trodden, and confused. In my prayers, I always ask God to think with my mind, to speak with my tongue, and to feel with my heart. I ask God to allow me to relate with the pain and the issues that the people are experiencing. A man and woman of God have to rely on God, the Holy Spirit, and his angels when doing the work of the Lord. Notice that I said the work of the Lord. To many times we find ourselves doing ministry and calling it working for the Lord. When you work for the Lord, you tend to want to receive some glorification for yourself. It is not about you. It is about the Lord. When you do the work of the Lord, then God gets all the glory. To God be the glory for the things he has done. He has done great things. I thank God for choosing me in this present time to share an encouraging word that will lift the burdens of many of his believing children. God's word also inspires me when my spirit gets low. That's why I can encourage my own self through scriptures. I can say to myself words like, I am more than a conquer through Christ Jesus. Greater is he that is in me than he that is in the world. I can do all things through Christ who strengthens me. No weapons formed against me shall prosper. To keep it personal, I can say; and we know that all things work together for the good of them that love the Lord and are called according to his purpose. It is important to know that God is able. As Jude said in Jude 1:24-25 (KJV)

Now unto him that is able to keep you from falling, and to present you faultless before the presence of his glory with exceeding joy, To the only wise God our Saviour, be glory and majesty, dominion and power, both now and ever. Amen.

God has been my keeper He has been with me through every facet of the ministry since day one.

ESCORTED BY AN ANGEL

One of the most difficult assignments that I had was visiting people that were in the hospital. Every visitation seemed different from the ones that I had done when I was a deacon. When I visited someone when I was serving as a deacon, they were eventually released from the hospital after a short stay. Now, when a visitation took place, it was as if I was the death angel from the television show Touched by an Angel. I can recall many occasions where this has happened. This frightened me to the point where I could not make those types of visits anymore. When I would visit someone, the person that I was visiting seemed as though they knew what their fate was going to be. The next day, or during church service, I would hear that the person had died. I asked when did he or she die and when they told me, a sadness came over me because that's the time I remember being with that person. On one occasion, I remember going to visit a young man that was in the hospital. When I stood by his bedside, he asked me why was I there. I told him that I was there to pray with him and to read a scripture from the Bible that would encourage him during his stay in the hospital. He asked me where the Bible was. I told him that I had it in my hand. He asked me if he could hold it. I told him yes. He said, what is in this Bible. I told him the word of God. He then took the Bible put it in his mouth and began to try and eat it. I asked him what he was trying to do. He replied that he was trying to get the Word of God in him. He later died the next day. During another visitation, I visited another young man at a different hospital. When I approached the nurses' station, they told me that the young man could not see because he was legally blind. When I entered the room, the young man asked who was present in the room with him. I told him that we were visiting from the church. I stated my name and my purpose for being there. The young man asked if I could give him a moment to pray before I began to minister to him. I told him whatever he wanted to do was fine with me. When the young man had finished praying, he began to recognize everyone in the room. Then he said something that everyone was stunned to hear. He said that he saw God in the room with him. He began to point with his finger across the room as if he was following the movement of someone passing through. The next day, I got word that the young man had died. Before my mother died in 1997, she had multiple strokes. Before her last stroke that left her speechless, she gave me some last minute motherly advice. One of the last things that mamma told me before she died is that she was not going to be with us very long. She told me that she was going to be in a better place and not to worry. One night, my oldest sister called me and told me that I needed to come to Georgia. She said that mamma had another stroke and the doctors said that she was not going to make it. She said that mamma was waiting for me to come see her. She also said that if anything were going to happen, it wouldn't happen until I got there. When I reached the hospital that night, I went to the waiting room. Everyone was expecting me. Then I went to mamma's room and held her hand. I thought about the things that she had recently told me. Then she died. Knowing what I know now makes it easier for me to deal with those that are dying and those that are grieving over the passing of a love one. Many times we pray and ask God to heal them and make them feel better. That is our will. We have to realize that life and death is in the hands of the Lord. When we pray, we should ask God to let his will be done and not ours. Now I know what my assignment is, so I just do what I have to do and not get upset about it because it's only God's will.

DREAM OF AN ANGEL

During the morning of Feb. 4, 2009, I was sound asleep. During the time that I was sleeping, I began to dream. I was dreaming of being an angel hovering over a crowd of people. Everyone saw me and was at awe, or was amazed. During my flight, I flew above the people with my hands outstretched talking and chanting. Suddenly my eyes arrested on a young mother with three children. I flew over to her and began to talk with her. I asked her did she believe. She was a little reluctant to answer. She said that she was having some difficulties taking care of herself and her children. So I gathered her and the children beneath my wings and assured her that everything was going to be okay. As I continued my flight, I was seen by a police officer at the door of a building. Immediately he pulled out his revolver, and began to utter something on his police radio. I flew down to him and asked him did he know who I was. He replied that he knew, but that I was causing a scene. Then I began to tell him that I was real. I proceeded to demonstrate to him the powers that were giving to me. I focused his attention on a marching crowd that was following a limousine. I told him to watch as I stopped the crowd in their steps. The limo continued to travel. I told him not to worry that the crowd would catch up. As we continued our conversation, somehow the police officer ended up chasing a guy carrying a weapon. They ran and eventually the guy was caught hiding in a trash dumpster. They tussled for a moment. The officer asked him where the gun was. Eventually he recovered a gun from the dumpster but told the officer that it was not his. The weapon was identical to the police revolver but was smaller. The flight continued with me flying over a bunch of young men that looked as if they were part of a gang. They looked at me and I looked at them with a stare letting them know that my eyes were on them. The bible even states that the eyes of the Lord are in everyplace beholding the good and the evil. Here are a few more dreams that I were able to record. On Feb. 15, I had a dream of this person that appeared to be my mother. Although I never got a look at her face, we had a long conversation about many things. That's how we spent our time together when she was living. One thing that we had talked about before she died in 1995 was for me to finish school. In this dream, I made a statement about school and her comments were this "Are you asking me a question?" I said to her, it's not a question. She said, "If it's going to make us some money, eighty to one-hundred thousand dollars then go for it." At that point the conversation ended. I remembered vividly after the conversation going and lying down on this very comfortable couch in a cozy comfortable room and began to relax. The furniture and the room was pure white. Then I woke up.

On Feb. 21, I had another dream that seem as though it was real. I dreamed of my baby sister and her son. In this dream I had a visit from my sister. She was telling me about her new place that she was living in. She told me to stop by and take a look at it. When I arrived at her place, it was all white as well. Her son opened the door so that I could come in. I could not see her and her son, but I was being led by a voice. When I got on the inside, everything on the inside was completely white. I heard as she told me that her room was up stairs. I followed the voice of her son up a very steep staircase. It seemed like we were climbing forever. It was as if I would never get to the end. When we reached the top of the staircase, there was no passage way to enter the room. The voice told me that I had to climb across a rail. When I began to put my foot across the rail, I stumbled and grabbed hold of the guard post. As I was holding on, it was as if I was going to fall, she said to me that I was not going to fall, just come on across. When I made it across, she said, "This is my room". While we were sitting there talking, she began to show me all kinds of precious and valuable jewelry. I had never seen anything like this before. Then she said to me, "It was his idea to get you to come visit us. She was referring to her son. The same thing happened here, I never saw their faces, but only heard their voices. Then I woke up. I believe without a shadow of a doubt that she is in heaven. This was the first visit, or should I say dream that I have had of them since that awful day. I also think that she just wanted me to know that she is in a good place and she has received her crowns. This dream came as a shocker because my sister, her son and the father of her children was killed in a horrific car accident in December of 2007. The driver of the other car also was killed. The only survivor of the accident was her sixteen year-old daughter who is left to bear the scars of this accident for the rest of her life. The night before the car accident happened, I had this dream where I laughed at something that was so hilarious, but I didn't remember what it was. The only thing that I remember from the dream is rolling over and pounding my hands to the ground in laughter. I told my wife about the dream, and she called me crazy. Later that night, I got a call from one of my nieces stating that my baby sister was killed in a car crash. I thought it was a joke until I got another call from the police department in Georgia saying that I needed to come to Georgia because I was a close relative of the deceased. Later my wife had told my mother-in-law about the dream that I had the day before. Her interpretation of the dream was that something terrible was going to happen.

On Feb. 24, 2009, I had quite a few dreams. Some of them are not that memorable. One of the dreams was about being at a function with a lot of people selling t-shirts. There was another dream where I was at a building that was being target for some type of crime. I remember hearing someone saying that the building was full of arsenic. Immediately I began to search for the substance and evacuate the building. I remembered trying to fly up through the ceiling of the building but found myself getting stuck in the attic. Then there appeared a man walking through the attic of the building. He said to me, "I knew you were going to try to come through here so let me help you. In my dreams I could feel the man lifting this heavy thing off of my shoulder making it possible for me to complete my task. It was like a heavy burden was lifted off of my shoulders. Then I woke up. The other dream was about a ceramic dog that was purchased by my wife. One day she was out shopping. She bought this ceramic dog and brought it home. She thought that I might like it because I love dogs. As I looked at the dog, it appeared to change into a human form. But there was something else interesting about the dog. The dog had a hollow inside. Inside the opening was another small stuffed animal with a name on it. I took both dogs back to the store where my wife had bought them. I asked the store clerk if she knew who the artist was that made them. The clerk remembered my wife buying the dog, but she didn't know who the artist was. I remembered leaving the dog on the outside of the store. When I looked out the window, the dog had changed into human form. It began to run, so I ran outside the store to catch it. It ran across the street, through the parking lot, into a building that had this beautiful Oceanside view. It was spectacular. There were beautiful white crescent waves beating against the boulder size rocks and the shoreline. Then I lost contact of the dog. That's when I awakened from my dream. On Feb. 26, 2009, I recorded another dream that I had dreamed during the early morning hours. In this dream, I was walking with my wife. We were talking and she said that she had something to show me. She said look up and behind the sun you will see a moon. As you know, no one can look directly in the sun with the natural eye. I looked up but I didn't see the moon where she said it would be. As I continued to look, we observed that there were many moons that were visible to the naked eye. Then I noticed that I was not walking on the ground, it appeared as if I was walking in space. Somehow, I was able to levitate in space. Again I woke in a state of awe. This was the second dream of this sort. I had a dream about being in space once before. I was on this planet that had a bright side and it had a dark side. I was told not to go on the dark side of the planet because if I did I would not be able to come back to the bright side. Because I was young and adventurous, I began to wander close to the dark side of the plant. Then I became curious. I wondered what would happen if I just stepped one foot across on the other side. When I put one foot on the dark side and had the other on the bright side, it was as if I were living on two different planets. I was stuck and couldn't free myself. The dark side of the planet was trying to pull me completely over on its side. Finally, the voice that told me not to venture over there came and freed me. It chastised me for being disobedient to the instructions that were given to me in the beginning. Once I was freed, I continued to explore the bright side of the planet with great joy.

After a few attempts of trying to record all my dreams, I grew weary. I felt as if I were losing too much sleep. Sometimes I could barely function when I arrived at work. My dreams of flying had subsided but, I continued to use what I had remembered in previous dreams. Whether they are dreams or a vision, they all seemed real. I do believe that there are some dreams that come true. Sometimes it seems as if you have been there before. The proper word for that is déjà vu.

On May 7, 2009, the dreams of flight reoccurred. This was another multiple flight dream where I appeared in many places. The first sighting was at a store. There was a woman at the store standing on the outside looking in. I didn't say anything to her because I already knew what was ailing her. I told the store owner that when she takes the initial step to enter the store to allow her get what she needed. It was up to her to make a decision. When she made her way inside the store, the store owner allowed her to get whatever she needed as much as she needed. She left the store joyfully telling others on her way. Jesus said in the book of Revelations, Behold I stand at the door and knock. If any man would open the door I would sup with him and he with me. When the others came to the store, it wasn't the same with them as it was with the woman. They had to pay for what they got. They couldn't understand why she got everything for free.

Then I journeyed to a small town in Georgia. There were two grieving women standing on the outside of a small church. Their main concern was not about the death of their love one, but about the welfare of a niece that was disobedient to their instructions. She was about to inherit a large sum of money and valuable property. Because of her lifestyle, they were afraid that she would continue to live a riotous life and swindle it all away. I talked to the young lady about the inheritance that she was about to receive and assured her that everything would be alright. When I approached the church, I encountered a very distinctive young man. The young man went into his closet and grabbed a robe. The robe was made of fine linen. It was purple and gold. Immediately, I said Q. Those were the colors of the fraternity of the brothers of the Omega Psi Phi fraternity. The conversation ended.

Next, I saw a man that I lived with for a few years. He was telling me that he had about fifty million dollars that were mine. He said that when he died he had left it for me and all I needed to do now is to get a lawyer and pursue actions to try and retrieve it. That was a very short dream, but it was intense.

Finally, I remember flying over an area secluded by trees. There were many people watching from below. They marveled at how I maneuvered through the air. As I flew lower through the trees, I got entangled in a very large web. It tried to hold me, but I was much too strong for it. I managed to loosen its grip and free myself. I continued on my flight.

In all the dreams that I had, they had a positive outcome. But, there were two dreams recorded in which I was unsuccessful in rescuing two individuals. The first one was about a young man being chased by several other young men. As he ran, I tried to shield him but I could not. Eventually he was caught by the other men. He pleaded for his life to no avail. One of the young men pulled out a gun. Then, I tried covering him to protect him from being shot. When the young man shot him, I felt as if I was shot myself. I could feel the pain and the agony of the young man. The young man curled up in a fetal position holding his hands on his chest. As the spirit left the body of the young man, I could feel every bit of it. My soul became vexed and I woke up feeling sad. I said to myself, some young man was killed tonight and I couldn't help him. The other dream was about a young lady that I heard screaming. When I reached her destination, she was surrounded by a gang of young men. I tried to intervene, but I couldn't no matter how hard I tried. The young men continued to harass her and all I could do was stand there and watch. They told me that there was nothing that I could do to help her. They continued by dragging her to a secluded area and continued their assault. It seemed as if I had lost all my ability to fly. I remember crawling to her rescue, but there was nothing that I could do.

On May 21, 2009, I had dreamed that I was flying. There were no heroics of any kind. I was just flying in a circular pattern praising and worshipping the Lord. I could remember having a feeling of joy, peace, and happiness.

DREAMS DO COME TRUE

Once I had a dream about the pastor of my church Dr. Robert C. Stanley, an associate minister Rev. Nathaniel Stevenson, and myself. Every time there was an engagement for the pastor, the three of us would always be there. After having this type of dream so many times, I decided to tell the pastor. He said that it might mean something. The final outcome was that the pastor needed an assistant pastor, and he ordained the associate minister as his assistant pastor, and I became very instrumental in assisting both of them. I am reminded of a scripture that's in the bible of a young man that had a dream and it came true. His name was Joseph. He was one of the sons of Jacob.

Genesis 37:5 (KJV) And Joseph dreamed a dream and he told it his brethren: and they hated him yet the more. And he said unto them, Hear, I pray you, this dream which I have dreamed: For, behold, we were binding sheaves in the field, and, lo, my sheaf arose, and also stood upright; and, behold, your sheaves stood round about, and made obeisance to my sheaf. And his brethren said to him, Shalt thou indeed reign over us? or shalt thou indeed have dominion over us? And they hated him yet the more for his dreams, and for his words. And he dreamed yet another dream, and told it his brethren, and said, Behold, I have dreamed a dream more; and, behold, the sun and the moon and the eleven stars made obeisance to me. And he told it to his father, and to his brethren: and his father rebuked him, and said unto him, What is this dream that thou hast dreamed? Shall I and thy mother and thy brethren indeed come to bow down ourselves to thee to the earth? This was a vision that Joseph had. His brothers called him a dreamer, but actually he was a visionary. Not only did he dream dreams, but he also had the ability to interpret dreams.

I had another dream of being taken up on the roof of this very tall building. While I was on the top of the building, I would begin to slide down, but something would push me back up. The voice said to me that I was not going to fall. I was not scared, but I was a little apprehensive. The voice said to me, "Take a look at the view. All this could be yours. All you have to do is to do my will." Immediately I woke up. This dreamed troubled me for a long time. I tried to get an understanding of the dream. I had no idea of what dreams meant. I did know that it had something to do with your subconscious mind while you are asleep. This only happens when you are in what psychologists call REM (rapid eye movement) sleep. I remembered reading when Jesus was tempted by Satin after fasting for forty days and taken up on a mountain top.

Matthew 4:1-11 (KJV) Then was Jesus led up of the Spirit into the wilderness to be tempted of the devil. And when he had fasted forty days and forty nights, he was afterward an hungred. And when the tempter came to him, he said, if thou be the Son of God, command that these stones be made bread. But he answered and said, It is written, Man shall not live by bread alone, but by every word that proceedeth out of the mouth of God. Then the devil taketh him up into the holy city, and setteth him on a pinnacle of the temple, And saith unto him, If thou be the Son of God, cast thyself down: for it is written, He shall give his angels charge concerning thee: and in their hands they shall bear thee up, lest at any time thou dash thy foot against a stone. Jesus said unto him, It is written again, Thou shalt not tempt the Lord thy God. Again, the devil taketh him up into an exceeding high mountain, and sheweth him all the kingdoms of the world, and the glory of them; And saith unto him, All these things will I give thee, if thou wilt fall down and worship me. Then saith

Jesus unto him, Get thee hence, Satan: for it is written, Thou shalt worship the Lord thy God, and him only shalt thou serve. Then the devil leaveth him, and, behold, angels came and ministered unto him.

Satan showed him everything and said this could be his if he did what he commanded. I could not put myself up there with Jesus; I could not put myself up there with God. I thought to myself, this sounds like something that Satin would do. Then I thought again, and said this could very well be the Lord showing me something. After mauling it over for a long period of time, I made a vow with the Lord. I believe that in that dream God was making a covenant with me and I promised the Lord that I would do whatever he asks me to do. Every since that day, I have been striving to live as holy as a sinner can live by the grace of God. I have been striving everyday to do the will of God. Since I have made that commitment, the Lord has never let me down. He has blessed me and my family. He has shown us how to be good stewards of the things that he has given us. We are able to support our local church with our time, talent, and treasure. From the words of David, Psalm 37:25 (KJV) I have been young, and now am old; yet have I not seen the righteous forsaken, nor his seed begging bread.

REALIZING YOUR PURPOSE

ack in the year of 1999, my wife and I had the opportunity to travel to Los Angeles California for a wedding. We stayed at a hotel in Long Beach for three nights and four days. We also traveled to Crenshaw, Compton, El Segundo and other neighboring towns. When you read about Los Angeles, you always hear of stories about graffiti, gangs and gang violence. I guess I had not gone to the right town because I didn't see any graffiti or gangs. Whenever I am in a different state, and living in a hotel, I am accustomed to getting up early every morning and working out. I don't care what state or city that I am in, I just enjoy my early morning workouts.

One particular morning while in LA, I decided to get up and go for a walk. I got up at 6 o'clock Florida time not realizing that it was 3 o'clock California time. I usually take a stroll around the hotel area to see what kind of eateries that is available. As I was walking from the hotel, I notice this young man behind me. My first thought was that he was part of a gang and I had crossed his turf. I continued to walk at a normal pace trying to get to the nearest building as possible without panicking. My second thought was that he was by himself and he really had to bring his "A" game if he tried something. With me weighing at that time around 230 pounds I didn't think he would try to attack me. I continued to walk towards the nearest store ahead which was a McDonalds. I said to myself, "If he tries to do something now, I would have a lot of witnesses. Just before entering the McDonalds, the young man manages to get my attention. He said that he had been up all night and that he was hungry. He wanted to eat something before he goes to school. I told him that I didn't have any money on me, but if he really wanted something to eat to come inside and I would pay for it with my credit card.

He told me that he wasn't allowed inside the store. I told him that I would tell them that he was with me. We proceeded to go into the store. The cashier asked, "How can I help you? I told her to take the young man's order and that I would pay for it. The young man placed his order which was not much. I asked him was that all he wanted and he hesitated. Then he asked if he could have more. I told him that he could have more if he wanted more. Then the cashier got over excited. She said, "I know who you are. I said' "You do not know me." She said, "Yes I do, you are that man that goes around helping people. I told her that I was not that man who she thought I was because I lived in Florida. That's when I truly realize what my purpose was. I guess that's why they call Los Angeles the city of Angels.

We do not know when the Lord is going to test us to see how we respond when someone approaches us that are in need. They could be angels in disguise. When we face Jesus Christ on the day of judgment, we all are going to have to give an account for every deed that we have done in this body whether it was good or bad. When Jesus asks us, what did you do concerning the building of the kingdom while you were living on earth?" We will have to confess. Every knee will have to bow and every tongue will confess.

Matthew 25:31-46 When the Son of man shall come in his glory, and all the holy angels with him, then shall he sit upon the throne of his glory: And before him shall be gathered all nations: and he shall separate them one from another, as a shepherd divideth his sheep from the goats: And he shall set the sheep on his right hand, but the goats on the left. Then shall the King say unto them on his right hand, Come, ye blessed of my Father, inherit the kingdom prepared for you from the foundation of the world: For I was an hungred, and ye gave me meat: I was thirsty, and ye gave me drink: I was a stranger, and ye took me in: Naked, and ye clothed me: I was sick, and ye visited me: I was in prison, and ye came unto me. Then shall the righteous answer him, saying, Lord, when saw we thee an hungred, and fed thee? or thirsty, and gave thee drink? [38] When saw we thee a stranger, and took thee in? or naked, and clothed thee? Or when saw we thee sick, or in prison, and came unto thee?] And the King shall answer and say unto them, Verily I say unto you, Inasmuch as ye have done it unto one of the least of these my brethren, ye have done it unto me. Then shall he say also unto them on the left hand, Depart from me, ye cursed, into everlasting fire, prepared for the devil and his angels: For I was an hungred, and ye gave me no meat: I was thirsty, and ye gave me no drink: I was a stranger, and ye took me not in: naked, and ye clothed me not: sick, and in prison, and ye visited me not. Then shall they also answer him, saying, Lord, when saw we thee an hungred, or athirst, or a stranger, or naked, or sick, or in prison, and did not minister unto thee? Then shall he answer them, saying, Verily I say unto you, Inasmuch as ye did it not to one of the least of these, ye did it not to me. And these shall go away into everlasting punishment: but the righteous into life eternal.

According Adam Clarke's Commentary on the New Testament, God will judge us concerning how we treat those that are less fortunately than others. He states that if men were sure that Jesus Christ was actually somewhere in the land, in great personal distress, hungry, thirsty, naked, and confined, they would doubtless run unto and relieve him. Now Christ assures us that a man, who is hungry, thirsty, naked, etc., is his representative, and that whatever we do to such a one he will consider as done to himself; yet this testimony of Christ is not regarded! Well, he will be just when he judges, and righteous when he punishes.

Lord, when saw we thee an hungered, etc.—It is want of faith which in general produces hard-heartedness to the poor. The man who only sees with eyes of flesh is never likely to discover Christ in the person of a man destitute of the necessaries of life. Some pretend not to know the distressed; because they have no desire to relieve them; but we find that this ignorance will not avail them at the bar of God.

COMPLETING THE VISION

Habakkuk 2:2-3 (KJV) And the Lord answered me, and said, Write the vision, and make it plain upon tables, that he may run that readeth it. For the vision is yet for an appointed time, but at the end it shall speak, and not lie: though it tarry, wait for it; because it will surely come, it will not tarry. Some people may think that I am just a dreamer when they read this book. I am not a dreamer, but a man with a vision.

Sometimes you may not be able to complete your visions. The vision may be completed in another generation. Moses saw the vision of going to the promise land that was filled with milk and honey. The promises were completed by Joshua forty years later. David had a vision to build a temple. The vision came true through his son Solomon. Dr. Martin Luther King Jr. had a vision. According to his Mountain Top speech, he was on a mission. One thing he said was that even though he had the vision, that he would not be able to complete the vision.

For years I have had a vision to help those that are not as fortunate as others. One of my biggest concerns is for young women. I grew up in a family of nothing but females. I lived with my six sisters and my mother for almost all my young adult life. I have witness the things that my sisters had to go through during their adolescence and into their adulthood. I also witness the turmoil that my mother went through trying to provide for her children. There are some things that I have witnessed that I cannot share in this book.

A few years after I accepted my call to the ministry, I had a dream of being the proprietor of this huge complex that would serve as a place of refuge for many women in the community. The complex consisted of state of the art buildings designed by me. One particular building had a bowling alley, sauna rooms, indoor track, basketball courts, an indoor swimming pool, and indoor handball courts. The building was also design with many classrooms that would be used for educational purposes. The other buildings were composed of units with rooms that would accommodate a fixed amount of women and their children if necessary. In my vision, it was not for me to make a profit, but that the women would have a place to recover until they are ready to go back to their normal lives. The vision was for a temporary stay with them giving a donation to the foundation if they had it. If they did not have it, they could still stay and go through the six months of rehabilitation and counseling.

The other vision that I have is to develop a program that would help our young children to develop and accomplish their goals. This was to be done by not taking over the normal responsibilities of the kids natural parents, but to enhance what they have already began to teach their kids. The vision of this program was called B.O.O.Y.S. (Building on Our Youths Strength). I believe by the help of God that these visions will come to fruition. R.Kelly may have written the lyrics to the song I believe I could fly. But if I could change one part of that song, it would be the part that says I think about it every night and day. I would change it to, I dream about it every night and day as I spread my wings and fly away. I believe I could soar. I see myself running through the open door. I know I can fly. In other words, I know I can succeed.

A Devine Intervention

On December 9, 2010, something very unusual happened to me. Two weeks prior to that date I had been experiencing episodes of shortness of breath. I thought this was due to me wearing a mask that was required by my place of employment. During this time of complications, my dog would sit and stare at me or would lie next to me never leaving my side. On the evening of Dec. 9, she jumped on me as she always did when she wanted to go for a walk. I ignored her because I didn't want to take her for a walk. A few minutes later she bumped me with her paw. I proceeded to get up, put her leash on and take her outside. It was wet and cold but I continued to take her for a walk. About two minutes into our walk, I began to have this tightness in my chest. It felt as if an elephant was standing on my chest. For a moment I could not breathe nor could I move. I stood in one spot hoping the pain would go away. Immediately out of nowhere came a strong wind. I could feel the wind as it encased me and felt as if it squeezed me. At that point I was able breathe again. I continued to walk my dog on our normal routine walk and returned home. I did not tell anyone about what had happened to me.

The next morning I went to work as usual feeling pretty good. Through the course of the day I began to feel exhausted. I could not walk or hold a conversation without getting tired. I was hoping the day would soon end so that I could go home. As time was approaching to clock out and go home, I could barely make it. I told my coworker that if I could just make it to my truck I would be okay. I managed to make it to the truck and drive home safely. Once I reached home, I sat on the couch for the remainder of the evening until my wife came home from work. She asked had I taken the dog for a walk. I told her no I did not. She said "Let's walk her together". I tried to convince her that I could not walk, but she kept on insisting that we do it together. Being the good husband that I am I tried to muster up enough energy to walk. We proceeded to take the dog for a walk. I forced myself to the point where I was too exhausted to make it back home. I struggled as I walked with excruciating pain and exhaustion. Once I reached home, I sat on the stoop in front of the house. At this point, she realized that something was really wrong with me. After resting for a few minutes, I managed to make it back into the house and lie down.

On Sunday Dec. 12, 2010, I pressed my way to church. There is something about being in the house of God. When I walked through the doors, tears began to roll down my cheeks. I was trying to figure out why I was crying so much. Immediately I began to praise and thank God for all that he had done for me. I realize that I could have been dead but by the grace of God he spared my life. I had so much to thank God for.

After service on that Sunday evening, my complications began to increase. Not only was I experiencing shortness of breath, buy now my left leg had begun to hurt. The pain was unbearable. I continued to struggle through it until my scheduled doctor's visit. When I finally saw the doctor on Dec.14, she immediately told me to go to the emergency room without hesitation. Upon arriving to the emergency room, various tests were run revealing multiple blood clots in both lungs and multiple clots in my left leg. Now the question was how I developed the clots in my lungs before I got them in my leg. I did not have any traumatic episodes, nor had I been on any extensive flights except those in my dreams. All I could say is that God is a miracle worker. God with his omnipotent powers dispersed his angels to minister to his servant. God divinely intervenes into our human affairs causing an outcome that only he can get the credit for. This is what we call a miracle. We should always give God the glory and honor for the things that he does in our lives. I was a dead man walking. We are constantly looking for God to perform miracles in our lives. Think of it this way, when God allows us to wake up to a see another day with the use and activity of our limbs that is a miracle. All those material things are just blessings. Jesus said seek yee first the kingdom of God and all these things will be added to you. Also, the bible says that if you delight yourself in the law of the Lord he will give you the desires of your heart.

MESSAGE OF AN ANGEL

When you look at all that is happening in the world today, you would agree with me that this world is in a terrible state. There are everything imaginable happening that I wouldn't be able to list them all. Here in the United States alone are enough problems that need to be focused on. In the United States we have HealthCare Issues, financial downfalls from major corporations. We are experiencing an economic downfall. Home foreclosures are at an all time high. People are losing jobs at an enormous rate. Thousands of young men and women are matriculating through college only to find It difficult to get a job. Many often move back home with their parents in hopes of finding their pursuit of happiness. More people are committing suicide because of family issues and loss of income. Domestic violence is increasing. Husbands and wives are killing one another and then committing suicide. The stock markets are inconsistent. The whole world is experiencing an economic downturn. Our troops are fighting what seems to me a never ending war.

The United States have elected an African American for president by the name of Barack Hussein Obama who is not welcomed by many, but many would like to see him fail. There are financial institutions going belly-up. We live in a country that was founded on the principles of God seems to have taken God out of the equation. We thrive on the words like God bless America. We even have on our money In God we trust. There are times when we pledge allegiance to a flag and say one nation under God. Do we really trust God? Are we really pledging our allegiance to God. Just like in the days of old, God is allowing things to happen so that his people will again learn how to lean and trust in him.

What we need to do as a country is to show the love for God and the love for our country that our fore founders had. God said in the Old Testament scriptures of:

2 Chron. 7:14 (KJV) If my people, which are called by my name, shall humble themselves, and pray, and seek my face, and turn from their wicked ways; then will I hear from heaven, and will forgive their sin, and will heal their land.

The second chapter of the book of Revelations shows us how God is holding the leaders, or angels of the localized churches responsible for the edifying of the people of God to do God's will. When Jesus comes back with his host of angels, we all are going to have to stand before the beamer and give an account of everything that we have done in this body whether it was good or bad. God is omnipotent. He has all power. He is omniscient. That means he knows all. He is omnipresent. God is everywhere at all times. He knows your every move every day. Jesus begins with each church by saying," I know thy works". Then he continues to tell them what he likes and dislike about what they are doing. Finally, He gives them a chance to correct their ways before he pass judgment. The word angel in this litany of scriptures refers to the pastors and leaders of the local church. Pastors are considered to be angels of the church that God has called them to pastor.

Jeremiah 3:15 And I will give you pastors according to mine heart, which shall feed you with knowledge and understanding.

Paul wrote to the church of Ephesus explaining the different gifts to the body of the local church.

Ephes. 4:11 And he gave some, apostles; and some, prophets; and some, evangelists; and some, pastors and teachers; Each church is represented differently and has a different message.

84

Rev. 2:1-5 says, Unto the angel of the church of Ephesus write; These things saith he that holdeth the seven stars in his right hand, who walketh in the midst of the seven golden candlesticks; I know thy works, and thy labour, and thy patience, and how thou canst not bear them which are evil: and thou hast tried them which say they are apostles, and are not, and hast found them liars: And hast borne, and hast patience, and for my name's sake hast laboured, and hast not fainted. Nevertheless I have somewhat against thee, because thou hast left thy first love. Remember therefore from whence thou art fallen, and repent, and do the first works; or else I will come unto thee quickly, and will remove thy candlestick out of his place, except thou repent.

Rev. 2:8-10 And unto the angel of the church in Smyrna write; These things saith the first and the last, which was dead, and is alive; I know thy works, and tribulation, and poverty, (but thou art rich) and I know the blasphemy of them which say they are Jews, and are not, but are the synagogue of Satan. Fear none of those things which thou shalt suffer: behold, the devil shall cast some of you into prison, that ye may be tried; and ye shall have tribulation ten days: be thou faithful unto death, and I will give thee a crown of life.

Rev. 2:12-18 And to the angel of the church in Pergamos write; These things saith he which hath the sharp sword with two edges; I know thy works, and where thou dwellest, even where Satan's seat is: and thou holdest fast my name, and hast not denied my faith, even in those days wherein Antipas was my faithful martyr, who was slain among you, where Satan dwelleth. But I have a few things against thee, because thou hast there them that hold the doctrine of Balaam, who taught Balac to cast a stumbling block before the children of Israel, to eat things sacrificed unto idols, and to commit fornication. So hast thou also them that hold the doctrine of the Nicolaitanes, which thing I hateRepent; or else I will come unto thee quickly, and will fight against them with the sword of my mouth. He that hath an ear, let him hear what the Spirit saith unto the churches; To him that overcometh will I give to eat of the hidden manna, and will give him a white stone, and in the stone a new name written, which no man knoweth saving he that receiveth it.

Rev. 2:18-29 And unto the angel of the church in Thyatira write; These things saith the Son of God, who hath his eyes like unto a flame of fire, and his feet are like fine brass; I know thy works, and charity, and service, and faith, and thy patience, and thy works; and the last to be more than the first. Notwithstanding I have a few things against thee, because thou sufferest that woman Jezebel, which calleth herself a prophetess, to teach and to seduce my servants to commit fornication, and to eat things sacrificed unto idols. And I gave her space to repent of her fornication; and she repented not. Behold, I will cast her into a bed, and them that commit adultery with her into great tribulation, except they repent of their deeds. And I will kill her children with death; and all the churches shall know that I am he which searcheth the reins and hearts: and I will give unto every one of you according to your works. But unto you I say, and unto the rest in Thyatira, as many as have not this doctrine, and which have not known the depths of Satan, as they speak; I will put upon you none other burden. But that which ye have already hold fast till I come. And he that overcometh, and keepeth my works unto the end, to him will I give power over the nations: And he shall rule them with a rod of iron; as the vessels of a potter shall they be broken to shivers: even as I received of my Father. And I will give him the morning star. He that hath an ear let him hear what the Spirit saith unto the churches.

Rev. 3:1-6 And unto the angel of the church in Sardis write; These things saith he that hath the seven Spirits of God, and the seven stars; I know thy works, that thou hast a name that thou livest, and art dead. Be watchful, and strengthen the things which remain, that are ready to die: for I have not found thy works perfect before God. Remember therefore how thou hast received and heard, and hold fast, and repent. If therefore thou shalt not watch, I will come on thee as a thief, and thou shalt not know what hour I will come upon thee. Thou hast a few names even in Sardis which have not defiled their garments; and they shall walk with me in white: for they are worthy. He that overcometh, the same shall be clothed in white raiment; and I will not blot out his name out of the book of life, but I will confess his name before my Father, and before his angels. He that hath an ear, let him hear what the Spirit saith unto the churches.

Rev. 3:7-14 And to the angel of the church In Philadelphia write; These things saith he that is holy, he that is true, he that hath the key of David, he that openeth, and no man shutteth; and shutteth, and no man openeth; I know thy works: behold, I have set before thee an open door, and no man can shut it: for thou hast a little strength, and hast kept my word, and hast not denied my name. Behold, I will make them of the synagogue of Satan, which say they are Jews, and are not, but do lie; behold, I will make them to come and worship before thy feet, and to know that I have loved thee. Because thou hast kept the word of my patience, I also will keep thee from the hour of temptation, which shall come upon all the world, to try them that dwell upon the earth. Behold, I come quickly: hold that fast which thou hast, that no man take thy crown. Him that overcometh will I make a pillar in the temple of my God, and he shall go no more out: and I will write upon him the name of my God, and the name of the city of my God, which is new Jerusalem, which cometh down out of heaven from my God: and I will write upon him my new name. He that hath an ear, let him hear what the Spirit saith unto the churches.

Rev. 3:14-22 And unto the angel of the church of the Laodiceans write; These things saith the Amen, the faithful and true witness, the beginning of the creation of God; I know thy works, that thou art neither cold nor hot: I would thou wert cold or hot. So then because thou art lukewarm, and neither cold nor hot, I will spue thee out of my mouth. Because thou sayest, I am rich, and increased with goods, and have need of nothing; and knowest not that thou art wretched, and miserable, and poor, and blind, and naked: I counsel thee to buy of me gold tried in the fire, that thou mayest be rich; and white raiment, that thou mayest be clothed, and that the shame of thy nakedness do not appear; and anoint thine eyes with eyesalve, that thou mayest see. As many as I love, I rebuke and chasten: be zealous therefore, and repent. Behold, I stand at the door, and knock: if any man hear my voice, and open the door, I will come in to him, and will sup with him, and he with me. To him that overcometh will I grant to sit with me in my throne, even as I also overcame, and am set down with my Father in his throne. He that hath an ear let him hear what the Spirit saith unto the churches.

In conclusion, we as men and women of God must share the unadulterated Gospel. God's word is infallible and God's word is true. I admire the instructions that Paul gave to Timothy. 2 Tim. 3:16-17 All scripture is given by inspiration of God, and is profitable for doctrine, for reproof, for correction, for instruction in righteousness: That the man of God may be perfect, thoroughly furnished unto all good works. 1 Thes. 2:4 says, But as we were allowed of God to be put in trust with the gospel, even so we speak; not as pleasing men, but God, which trieth our hearts. Galatians 1:10 say, For do I now persuade men, or God? or do I seek to please men? for if I yet pleased men, I should not be the servant of Christ. 2 Tim. 4:2 says, Preach the word; be instant in season, out of season; reprove, rebuke, exhort with all longsuffering and doctrine. These are my sentiments as well. We all must make a stand when it comes to the word of God. We must denounce sin no matter who it's in. This holds true and evident to those who believe and are called to do God's will. I am a firm believer that when you commit yourself to being obedient to the Lord, there is no good thing that he will withhold from you.

As a messenger of God, or one of God's angels; I would like to encourage everyone to search their souls and find your way back to God. God has never stopped pouring out his blessings upon those that are loyal to him. God will supply all your needs and make a way out of no way. When things look dim, God will shine a light on that situation and make your way more pleasant. God said that he will not put any more on you than you can bear. And if you think that you are going to perrish, I read about what David said in Psalm 37:25 I have been young, and now am old; yet have I not seen the righteous forsaken, nor his seed begging bread. God will take care of you. I am living proof of what God can do. There are times when my wife tells me that I don't worry about anything. Why should I worry when Jesus said not to worry? In Matthew 6:25 Jesus said it this way. Therefore I say unto you, Take no thought for your life, what ye shall eat, or what ye shall drink; nor yet for your body, what ye shall put on. Is not the life more than meat, and the body than raiment? Jesus went on to say consider the birds how they don't work nor do they have a place stay. Yet every day the bird gets up and find whatever that is suitable for them to eat. In other words, if He takes care of a bird are we much greater than a bird. I don't know about you, but I am better than a bird. And if God has his eye on the sparrow, I know that he has an eye on me.

Matthew 6:26 Behold the fowls of the air: for they sow not, neither do they reap, nor gather into barns; yet your heavenly Father feedeth them. Are ye not much better than they? When I had that mountain top experience in my dream, I made a vow or covenant to the Lord that I would do whatever he ask me to do. Not only did I make that vow in my dream, but I also made the same vow in reality. In return God assured me that he would supply all my needs. So if God said it that settles it. Don't you try to do what God can do? It's not up to you. Leave it in the hands of the Lord. I know that everyday there is a challenge. Instead of looking at your problems as difficult issues, consider them as opportunities for character development. This is often quoted by Pastor Eric Jones of the Koinonia Worship Center. One thing that I have done is to put my trust in God. I have accomplished this by strengthening my relationship with God. One way of strengthening your relationship with God is by committing yourself to the word of God, the will of God and the way of God.

In Exodus 16:28 The Lord said to Moses, "How long will you refuse to do what I have commanded and instructed you to do? In John 14:15 Jesus said, If ye love me, keep my commandments. My brothers and my sisters, God will impart his blessings upon those who are obedient to him. You will be blessed in the city and blessed in the field. Everything that you set out to do shall be blessed. God will make you a lender and not a borrower. He shall make you the head and not the tail. We need to understand that our blessings are connected to our obedience.

May God continue to bless and keep you.

This poem is written based on the things that I have witnessed in the neighborhoods and the actions of some of our young men and women. It is not intended to insult or to degrade anyone.

Hold on a change is going to come

Young men born with no state of mind
Blind to the ways of mankind
They ain't got no money they ain't got no job
They just walk around town looking like a slob
Hold on a change is going to come

Middle-aged men sitting under a tree
They only get up when it's time to pee
Playing dominoes just to pass the time
They need to be at work trying to make a dime
Hold on a change Is going to come

Many young girls trying to look like Divas
If they only knew that they are only deceivers
Wearing male clothes like Peppermint Paddy
You can't tell if they're the momma or the baby daddy
Hold on a change is going to come

Many of the mothers are not making wise decisions
It's all about the looks and not the provisions
They have bad attitudes like carrying guns and knives.
It stems from watching realty shows or being desperate house wives
Hold on a change is going to come

BIBLIOGRAPHY

Hammond, Frank and Ida Mae. Pigs in the Parlor. Missouri: Impact Books, 1973

National Council on Child and Family Violence Retrieved 9 February 2009, from, http://www.nccafv.org/spouse.htm

Strong, James New Strong's Exhaustive Concordance of the Bible, Thomas Nelson Publishing 1990

WORDsearch 9 Thompson Chain-Reference Bible Library, Wordsearch Corp.